The SPORTS HEROES Library

Basketball's
POWER PLAYERS

Nathan Aaseng

 Lerner Publications Company • Minneapolis

To Sharla, Solveig, Lynn, and Marty

LIBRARY OF CONGRESS CATALOGING IN PUBLICATION DATA

Aaseng, Nathan.
 Basketball's power players.

 (The Sports heroes library)
 Summary: Profiles eight pro basketball players who
are experts at rebounding, playing defense, and driving
to the basket: Moses Malone, Maurice Lucas, Jack Sikma,
Adrian Dantley, Jeff Ruland, Buck Williams, Dan
Roundfield, and Terry Cummings.
 1. Basketball players—United States—Biography—
Juvenile literature. [1. Basketball players] I. Title.
II. Series.
GV884.A1A243 1985   796.32'3'0922 [B]   84-21859
ISBN 0-8225-1342-0 (lib. bdg.)

Manufactured in the United States of America

International Standard Book Number: 0-8225-1342-0
Library of Congress Catalog Card Number: 84-21859

1 2 3 4 5 6 7 8 9 10 94 93 92 91 90 89 88 87 86 85

Contents

Moses Malone (24) knows that it will take muscle and determination to keep Kareem Abdul-Jabbar from scoring at will.

4

Introduction

Basketball is a noncontact sport, right? Don't the rules say that if you so much as bump someone, you can be whistled for a foul? By reading the rulebook and by watching highlight films, one gets the idea that basketball is a game only for speedsters, graceful gliders and leapers, and dead-eye shooters. Big muscles don't seem to count for anything.

Try telling that to a pro basketball center who can't even begin to count the number of bumps and bruises on his body at the end of a game! An evening of shoving, leaning, hip-banging, and mid-air crashes leaves him exhausted. Make no mistake about it: the pro game is rough! Although the spinning lay-ups may look pretty, many coaches insist that it's the scrapping under the basket that usually decides the game.

There are three areas of the game in which brute power and stubborn determination count: rebounding, defense, and driving to the basket. While none of these skills wins much notice from fans, they are appreciated by coaches and players. Larry Bird, Boston's high-scoring forward, has said that grabbing 20 rebounds is more important than scoring 35 points. Each rebound means one more shot for your team or one less for the other guys. Although it would seem that players who can reach and jump the highest would get the most rebounds, it doesn't work that way. Among the National Basketball Association's top ten rebounders in 1982-83, there were none who were seven feet or taller. Instead, the battle for rebounds is won by getting good position and by blocking foes to keep them from getting close to the basket.

Strength, quickness, and hard work are defensive skills needed to cool off the NBA's hot scorers. For example, if a player like Kareem Abdul-Jabbar is able to roam near the basket, he will wear out the netting with easy baskets. The key to stopping players like Jabbar is to keep them away from the rim, and that means a lot of leaning and blocking.

Finally, many NBA points are scored by those who can muscle their way to the basket. A powerful player can back his opponent under the net and then force his shot through a web of arms toward the hoop.

This bird's-eye shot of 1981 NBA championship action shows the Boston Celtics and the Houston Rockets fighting for control of pro basketball's most important space: those few feet in close to the basket.

The men in this book have changed the impression that pro basketball players are overpaid artists who don't give much effort. Pro basketball championships are won by hard-working people such as Moses Malone, Maurice Lucas, and Jack Sikma who help their team every night by outworking, outbattling, and outmuscling their opponents. They, along with the five others in this book, have shown how badly pro teams need an overpowering force to take control of that no-man's land around the basket.

Although he's a millionaire, Philadelphia's Moses Malone still has to sweat for a living!

1

Moses Malone

"Wear out the big guy" is one of basketball's favorite strategies when playing against a large, star center. Big people can't lug their massive bodies up and down the court the way the little guys can. So the opposition makes them work hard on defense, leaning on them to make them work for their points and racing up and down the court.

No team tries that against big Moses Malone, however. If they did, they might wind up with 12 players in an oxygen tent while Moses just kept on rolling along! Malone is the best example of what muscle, endurance, and plain hard work can do for a basketball player. Combined with his natural skill, it has made him one of the top players in the game.

Moses was born in Petersburg, Virginia, in 1956. As a boy, he preferred football to other sports. Pro linemen, however, can be thankful that Malone switched to basketball at the age of 13. At first, his appearances at the local playground games were embarrassing. He was awkward, and his small hands made it hard for him to latch onto the ball. But he wasn't discouraged when others laughed at him. He just kept practicing—and growing!

By the time Moses reached high school, he was a well-coordinated, 6-foot, 10-inch center who completely bullied opponents on the court. During his final two years, he averaged 36 points, 25 rebounds, and 10 blocked shots per game. He had also learned that basketball was a team sport, and he blended well enough with his teammates to help Petersburg win 50 straight games while capturing two state championships.

Long before graduation, Moses found himself swarmed by college recruiters. After sorting out hundreds of confusing offers, Malone chose to attend the University of Maryland. Just before starting classes, however, Moses shocked the sports world by turning pro. The 18-year-old signed a contract with the Utah Spurs of the American Basketball Association (ABA).

As the first basketball player to enter the pro ranks out of high school, Moses had a lot to learn. It had been easy for him to score on lay-ups and dunks against smaller high school centers. But suddenly he had to go up against veteran pros who were as big or bigger than he was. Malone hurt his team with his poor passing and ball-handling.

Despite his disappointing performance, Moses' Utah teammates immediately noticed something certain to make him a star. Despite his size, Malone could move as quickly as the team's guards, which meant he could often slip past the slower-footed men who guarded him. Malone handled the difficult jump to the pros with an 18.8 scoring average and 14.6 rebounds per game in 1975-76. But money problems forced the Spurs out of business and started Moses on a frustrating trip around the country. He played for the St. Louis Spirits in 1976-77; then St. Louis went out of business, and he was claimed by Portland. Portland quickly dealt Malone off to Buffalo, and they kept him less than a week before trading him to Houston.

Finally settled with the Rockets, Malone set about doing what he could do better than anyone else in the history of basketball. During his first season, he grabbed 437 offensive rebounds to set an NBA record in that category. Offensive rebounds, those gathered when a teammate misses a shot, are especially tough to get. Most pros use their muscle and size to block out offensive players so they never get near the backboard, but Moses was quick enough to scoot around and strong enough to break through. He tried hard for every rebound, sometimes tipping the ball in the air two or three times before gaining control.

Despite his offensive rebounding, in 1977-78 there were doubts that Moses would ever be a dominating center like Bill Russell or Kareem Abdul-Jabbar. In 1978-79, Malone answered his critics by bearing down even harder. He averaged an astounding 17.6 rebounds per game, including 587 off the offensive boards, and was named the Most Valuable Player in the NBA. The next season, Moses moved into the ranks of the top scorers with a 27.8 average and continued to rebound well, averaging 14.8 per game. Malone's constant hustle moved his coach to stop practice once to shake his star center's hand.

Despite Malone's efforts, the Rockets stumbled to a 40-42 record in 1980-81, and few fans gave them much chance in the play-offs against the defending champion Los Angeles Lakers. But Malone went to work and so controlled the rebounding that the Rockets pulled off the upset. Then after crushing the Kansas City Kings with a performance that included one game of 42 points and 23 rebounds, Malone led his team into the finals against the Boston Celtics. Despite playing with just an average

Moses displays the kind of extra effort that powered the lowly Rockets to the 1981 championship finals against Boston.

13

team, Malone forced the Celtics to six games before losing the series, four games to two. Far from being burned out from his tireless efforts over a long season, Malone was ready to go again a week after the season ended. The sport may have been a business to some, but for Moses, it was "just playin' ball."

In 1981-82, Malone proved that he was in the same class as the best centers who had ever played. By grabbing 14.7 rebounds per game, he became the first player since Wilt Chamberlain to win the NBA rebounding title two years in a row. At the same time, he boosted his scoring average to 31.1.

The Philadelphia 76ers looked at those numbers and decided that Malone was just what they needed to finally nail down a title. Although loaded with talent, the 76ers had kept coming up short in the play-offs. They were willing to part with center Caldwell Jones, a number-one draft choice, and a mind-boggling amount of money to get the man who could bring them a title.

There were some who claimed the 76ers would regret the deal and that stars like Julius Erving and Andrew Toney might not enjoy being pushed into the shadows by their new teammate. But Malone had only one thing on his mind—a championship.

When the 76ers brought in Malone (2) to face off against Boston's Robert Parish (00), the Boston-Philadelphia rivalry *really* began to heat up!

Moses Malone

He was happy to let the others shoot as often as they wanted. "Don't worry about getting the ball to me," he said. "I'll go to the boards."

Not only did the 76ers appreciate Moses' rebounds and unselfish play, they also started to copy his playing style. The whole team began to work harder and to play more aggressively. Malone pounded away against the strongest centers in the game and usually had them worn out by the fourth

16

quarter. The recharged 76ers sprinted to a 50-7 record before coasting to a 65-17 finish, the fourth best mark in NBA history.

When asked how he thought the play-offs would go that year, Malone answered simply, "Four, four, and four." He meant that his team would win each of their series in four straight games. The center missed on his prediction by only one game when the 76ers won 12 of their 13 play-off games, the best NBA play-off showing ever. Malone's trophy case became crammed as he earned his fourth rebounding title in five years, the Most Valuable Player Award for the season, and the Most Valuable Player Award for the play-offs. While the 76ers failed to hold on to their championship in 1983-84, Malone continued to make history by winning his fourth straight NBA rebounding title.

Although proud of these accomplishments, Moses is prouder yet of one thing. He thinks of himself as the hardest working player in the game, and he intends to keep it that way. As long as he does, the only way to keep him away from the basket is with a crow bar!

When a man wants a rebound as badly as fiery Maurice Lucas does, even Moses Malone (24) has to be wary!

2
Maurice Lucas

Maurice Lucas is a man of peace. He hates violence and spends most of his time in calm, quiet activities. Along with Bill Walton, Lucas was one of the few athletes to switch to a vegetarian diet. It hardly seems possible that this mild-mannered man has also been the most-feared player in basketball. Powerfully built at 6 feet, 9 inches and 220 pounds, Lucas plays the game as if he were searching for the man who had burned down his house. Strong men shy away from shoving matches with him, and, if Lucas starts one, they push back warily. Maurice's blend of skill, power, and fury has made him the classic example of a power forward.

Maurice was born in Pittsburgh, Pennsylvania, in 1952. It wasn't the happiest of childhoods, however, as his father died when Maurice was six.

As a skinny kid in a tough neighborhood, Lucas had to scrap to survive, and he fell into such bad ways as robbing fruit stands.

When it came to basketball, little Maurice figured he would have to scrap just as hard. The scrawny 6-foot sophomore at Schenley High School in Pittsburgh ran up the hills around school to get in shape and learned to dive for loose balls in practice.

Before his junior year, Lucas suddenly sprouted seven inches and began to fill out as well as up. It was embarrassing for him because he had no money to buy new clothes and had to stretch his socks to get them to reach the bottom of his pants. But his size helped him in basketball. A 6-foot, 9-inch player battling with the desperation of a little guard made college coaches take notice. Of the coaches he talked to, Maurice liked Marquette University coach Al McGuirre the best. McGuirre was one of the few coaches who liked emotional players, and that suited Lucas fine.

At Marquette, Maurice put in some hard work as a rebounder. There was something about his menacing look that made opponents step lightly around him. In 1974, he powered the Warriors to the finals of the NCAA tournament, where they fell to North Carolina State.

With the tournament experience under his belt, Lucas skipped his senior year of college to join the pros. Along with another power forward, Marvin Barnes, he signed with the St. Louis Spirits of the ABA. Although Maurice averaged more than 10 rebounds per game, he had to work in the shadow of Barnes, who won the ABA Rookie of the Year Award. Lucas moved on to Kentucky the next year. There, despite quarrels with his coach, he averaged 17 points and 12 rebounds per game. Those two years in the ABA also earned him a reputation as a madman. Feeling that rebounding was a state of mind, Lucas spent hours before a game working himself into a fury. Sometimes he overdid it, however, which led to fights with people as huge as 7-foot, 2-inch Artis Gilmore and as gentle as Julius Erving.

In 1976, the ABA merged with the NBA, and Lucas, was one of the ABA players put into a special draft. He was chosen by the Portland Trail Blazers, and that was a lucky break for both. There Lucas teamed up with injury-prone center Bill Walton to form the best rebounding combination in the league.

With Portland, Maurice was willing to run the entire game in order to get away from defenders.

21

Portland teammate Bill Walton thanked Lucas for his defensive help by feeding him sharp passes, which helped Maurice fatten his scoring average.

As soon as Lucas broke free, Walton's sharp passes would set him up for a score. This helped Maurice to the best scoring seasons of his career in 1976-77, a 20.2 average. In return, Lucas protected Walton from the pounding he had been taking from beefier players. One fierce glare from Lucas, and opponents scrapped any plans of taking it to Walton.

Portland blazed all the way to the finals of the 1977 play-offs. There they had problems with Philadelphia and were blown out of the first two games. In game two, enormous Darryl Dawkins challenged a smaller Blazer to a fight, and Lucas rushed in swinging. Afterwards, Maurice felt embarrassed by his actions and made a point of shaking hands with Dawkins in front of the Philadelphia bench before game three. Proving he was the best power forward in the league, Lucas then went on to help Portland sweep the next four games.

Portland played even better the next year, and their average margin of victory grew to more than 10 points per game. Lucas provided the muscle to give the team a perfect blend of defense, rebounding, shooting, and passing. But a wave of injuries struck and ruined the Portland powerhouse. When Walton went to the sidelines, a hobbling Lucas was forced to carry the load. That year, he came through with a 20.4 scoring average and a 10.4 rebounding mark, but Portland failed to repeat their championship.

Portland wasted no time in deciding to rebuild their team and traded Maurice to the New Jersey Nets. After a brief stint there, Lucas joined the

Maurice Lucas

New York Knicks, where injuries continued to hold down his production.

In 1982, the Phoenix Suns were trying to figure out why things kept going sour for them in the play-offs. Although one of the top teams in the NBA, the Suns never went far in post-season play. They finally decided they didn't have enough muscle to stand up to the bigger teams and went after Maurice Lucas to solve that problem.

The Suns' new forward makes it clear to the Chicago Bulls' Dwight Jones that his team is not going to be pushed around anymore.

Bolstered by their new power forward, the confident Suns moved into the play-offs. But Lucas went to the sidelines with a leg problem in game two of their series with Denver, and suddenly the Suns were out of the running again. Maurice recovered and finally regained his standing as one of the top rebounders in the league in 1983-84. Then Lucas proved that the Suns had known what they were doing when they had wanted him for the play-offs. Playing with that same barely-controlled rage he had shown back in 1977, Maurice powered his team past favored Utah and gave the mighty Los Angeles Lakers a scare before bowing out in the Western Conference finals. Although the Suns still couldn't seem to win it all, at least life was a bit easier for them. With Lucas on their side, life was a lot safer under the basket than it had been before.

3
Jack
Sikma

Pro scouts may never forgive Jack Sikma for what he has done to them. Sikma wasn't like a Larry Bird or a Magic Johnson, whom scouts were certain would be stars. Then again, he wasn't one of the Three Stooges, either. Jack was one of those borderline cases, and the pros could only guess about him. Their best guess was that while he might be a sound player, he was probably too frail to be a star.

Within two years, Sikma had totally embarrassed the scouts. It was bad enough that he had blossomed into a star. But Sikma had earned his points and rebounds by winning the banging and shoving matches in the lane. Calling Sikma too frail was like saying Abdul-Jabbar was too short to be a pro center!

27

Try telling a beleaguered Kareem Abdul-Jabbar (33) that Jack Sikma
(43) is too frail to stand up to pro centers!

Jack was born in Kankakee, Illinois, in 1955. He grew up 60 miles south of Chicago, helping his dad farm and raise flowers. Like Maurice Lucas, Sikma learned his basketball as a short guard. Just a shade over six feet when he entered St. Anne High School, he had to master the shooting and passing skills that smaller players need to compete.

As Sikma started growing, he learned the other positions on the court, first as a 6-foot, 4-inch forward and then as a 6-foot, 9-inch center. Even at that height, he seemed to have little future in the game. College coaches took one look at the thin lad and pictured him getting bounced around like a ping pong ball at the college level.

Sikma finally settled on a small school, Illinois Wesleyan University. With only 1,600 students and no great basketball tradition, the school seemed a poor place to train for the pros. But Jack was free to improve at his own pace and to do some experimenting. At Wesleyan, he invented a move that helped him to get off shots against the best defensive centers. Jack would sweep one foot in front of the other to keep the defender back on his heels. Then he would take his jump shot. With his long arms firing from far behind his head, Sikma's shot could not be blocked. Some coaches were so impressed with Jack's progress that they talked of him as a great Olympic prospect in 1976. But even though the team was weakest at center, Jack was not asked to join the U.S.A. squad.

The Seattle Supersonics was one of many pro teams to wonder whether Jack had the strength to make it as a pro center, but they decided his shooting and passing skills were too good to pass up. Sikma was their number-one draft choice in 1976, and he was expected to learn his trade as a backup center to Marvin Webster.

After the Supersonics staggered to a 5-17 start that season, they decided to make drastic changes. Rookie Sikma was put into the lineup at a new position, forward. The quiet, polite Sikma was a coach's dream as he listened carefully to instructions and played hard every night. He seemed so happy to have made the team that he did whatever was asked of him.

The switch worked well for both Seattle, which advanced to the NBA championship finals, and for Sikma, who made the NBA All-Rookie team. Jack showed there was plenty of strength in his 6-foot, 11-inch, 230-pound body, and once he discovered that pushing and shoving was a way of life in the pros, he was willing to stand up to anyone.

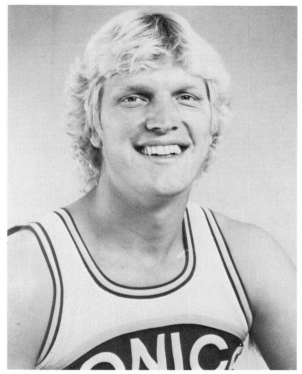

Jack Sikma

Jack was still trying to master his new position in 1978 when the Sonics suddenly needed a center. With Webster moving on to the New York Knicks and Tom LaGarde injured, Sikma was asked to move back to the middle. Scouts who had expected him to get chewed up in the land of the giants were stunned when Jack averaged 12.3 rebounds per game. In fact, the centers he had the most trouble with were the smaller, less punishing ones. In the play-offs, Jack fell into a six-game slump against quick Alvan Adams of Phoenix. But he finally pulled out of it to score 33 points in the key seventh game to keep his team in the title chase.

Seattle moved on to the finals for a rematch against the defending champion Washington Bullets. There Jack faced Wes Unseld, the most bruising center in the game and the championship series' Most Valuable Player the year before. This time, however, Sikma was the one throwing his weight around. He scored and blocked shots and even outrebounded Wes, grabbing 17 rebounds in each of the final three games. With such an edge at the key center position, Seattle won the title easily. In only two years, Jack had gone from being an unsure rookie to being the rugged leader of the NBA's best team.

Although his team did not repeat as champions, Sikma kept improving and gave the Sonics steady performances in nearly every game. His best season was in 1981-82 when he scored 19.6 points per game and finished second in the league in rebounds with 12.7. That season, he became one of the few centers to play Moses Malone to a standoff in post-season play. With 30 points and 17 rebounds against Malone, Sikma and the Sonics bounced Houston out of the play-offs.

Here Jack loses a ball to master rebounder Wes Unseld of the Bullets. Sikma, however, outmanuevered Unseld consistently in this 1978 championship series as Seattle won its first NBA title.

Sikma's tireless efforts to gain position under the basket pay off as he cradles a rebound he has snatched away from Boston's Rick Robey.

By 1982-83, the quiet center had taken his place as one of the NBA's top all-around performers. Twice that season, he gathered 25 rebounds in a game, which was tops in the league. Jack also became the first center in almost 20 years to finish in the top ten in free throw shooting with a sizzling 85.5 percent, a feat he duplicated in 1983-84. Rounding out his game, Jack continued to hand out his career average of three assists per game.

Who would have guessed that "frail" Jack Sikma would be known among his teammates as "Banger?" That was a fitting nickname for the man who took just six years to become Seattle's all-time leading rebounder and is adding on to his record with every game he plays.

When Adrian Dantley charges to the hoop, not even a jarring collision
with a Celtic forward can throw him off stride.

4
Adrian
Dantley

Basketball experts like to divide NBA forwards into two types, power forward and small forward. The power forward is a bruising, 6-foot, 10-inch strongman who can play defense and control rebounds. The small forward is a quick 6-foot, 7-inch player who can run and shoot. Most say that to be successful, a team must have one of each kind.

Meet Adrian Dantley, the man who turned this theory into utter nonsense. The star forward of the Utah Jazz stands only 6 feet, 5 inches, which shouldn't even qualify him as a small forward. Yet his game of power and muscle has turned him into one of the game's top scorers.

Adrian was born in Washington, D.C., in 1956. He grew up watching a powerful small forward named Elgin Baylor dazzle crowds at suburban

DeMatha High School. Baylor went on to star in the pros, and his old high school kept turning out star players in the Baylor mold. For more than 20 years, every senior on the DeMatha team earned a college basketball scholarship. But none of them was as widely praised as stocky Adrian Dantley.

Dantley worked hard to become as good as Baylor. When his friends begged him to go out with them on a Friday night, Adrian would insist on working out by himself on a basketball court under the lights. This hard work brought Adrian a scholarship to Notre Dame University. As a freshman, he helped the Irish break UCLA's record 88-game winning streak, averaging 18 points per game. Despite these successes, however, Adrian was miserable most of the time. His junk food diet had made him somewhat pudgy, and opponents kept telling him how fat he was. This bothered Adrian so much that he went on a crash diet, which caused him to collapse during a game. Dantley grew homesick and asked to be excused from practices so he could catch up on his homework.

After trying a more reasonable diet, Adrian returned for his sophomore year, thinner and more confident. He won All-American honors two years in a row and was named a starter for the 1976

Adrian Dantley

U.S.A. Olympic team. The American squad had no dominating center nor any true power forwards, so it was up to the 6-foot, 5-inch Dantley to provide the inside offense. This he did, muscling his way past larger players to score 30 points in the team's gold medal win over Yugoslavia. With the gold medal in his hands, Dantley skipped his junior year at Notre Dame to join the pros.

It was a blow to Adrian's pride when five players were selected before him in the 1976 draft. But despite his efforts over the previous two years, Dantley had never silenced his critics. They still said he was too fat, too short, and too slow to be a star and that his body wasn't suited for any pro position.

True, Dantley was still stocky, but that was because of a massive, 43-inch chest instead of fat. Built like a fullback, Dantley showed that he could play like one, too. It didn't matter that he was shorter than other players because he didn't have to go over them. Instead, he could back in on them and force his way to the hoop. Once near the basket, Dantley's great balance allowed him to change his shot in midleap. Many of his shots snaked through the mass of arms blocking his way while Adrian drew a foul. He was so good at making opponents foul him that a third of his points came from shooting free throws.

The Buffalo Braves found out what kind of a player their rookie was when he led them in scoring with a 20.3 average in 1977 and earned NBA Rookie-of-the-Year honors. Still he was traded to Indiana the next season and then was sent on to the Los Angeles Lakers a couple of months later. People couldn't get used to a man who didn't fit the usual catagories of small or power forward.

Like the rest of the NBA, Julius (Dr. J) Erving (6) couldn't figure out what to do with Buffalo's undersized strongman.

The Lakers tried to make a power forward of Adrian, but power forwards need to play great defense, which wasn't Dantley's strong suit. Also, power forwards are not expected to do much scoring, which *was* his strong point. After his average fell to 17.3 in 1978-79, Dantley was happy to be packing his bags again, even if it meant being traded from a good team to the laughable Utah Jazz. At least with the Jazz, "AD" could play his game, and he saved one of his best demonstrations, a 50-point outburst, for his old Laker teammates. In his unspectacular way, Dantley worked for position, drew fouls, and backed in for close shots. The Jazz, who got little scoring from their big men, counted on the short forward for their inside offense.

Although the Jazz kept losing, Adrian worked his way up to the top of the scoring charts. He averaged 28.0 points in 1979-80, a league-leading 30.7 the next year, and 30.3 in 1981-82. Adrian seemed to be on his way toward greater heights the following year when he scored 57 points in a game early in the year. But a torn ligament in his wrist put him on the bench for all but 22 games.

When Dantley returned, everything was back to normal, and he kept collecting "garbage" baskets near the hoop as well as long shots from the outside.

By blasting into the heart of the defense—in this case Boston's Larry Bird and Robert Parish—Dantley became the fourth person in NBA history to score more than 800 points from the foul line in a single season.

The Jazz experimented with him at several positions, including guard, and Adrian kept coming up with his 30 points a game. He continued to bang around in heavy traffic underneath the basket and drew more fouls than any other player in the league. The pounding paid off, however, as Dantley was able to sink over 200 more free throws than any other NBA player in 1983-84. Those free throws allowed him to win the league scoring title that year, his second in four years.

The only change for Dantley that year was that the Jazz finally started winning. With their husky forward leading the way, Utah surprised everyone by winning their first divisional title that season. Utah's star fullback—er, forward—had shown that you don't have to fit the mold to be a winner and that there's more than one way to get to the basket.

5
Jeff
Ruland

For many years, Washington Bullet opponents looked forward to the day when Wes Unseld would retire. They had been bounced around by the Bullets' block of granite until they were dizzy, and they had the bruises and welts to show for it.

When husky Wes did retire before the 1982 season, players expected a more peaceful game when they visited the Landover, Maryland, arena. Instead, they found a man who was four inches taller than Unseld, a few pounds heavier, and light years beyond him as a shooter. They quickly realized there would be no relief in sight as long as Washington's surprising star, Jeff Ruland, was planted under the basket.

Ruland's ability to muscle in for close shots enabled him to hit a sizzling 57.9 percent in 1983-84.

Jeff was born on Long Island, New York, in 1958 Everyone in his neighborhood got along so well that Ruland didn't have any white friends until sixth or seventh grade. When Jeff was nine, his father died, and his mother was kept busy running a bar to earn a living. Jeff was left on his own far more than most children, and it would have been easy for him to get into trouble. But he was a "great kid," according to his mom, and it didn't occur to him to get too far out of line. Besides, he was too interested in basketball to get involved in anything else.

Ruland practically camped out on the neighborhood courts. Even during the snows of January, Jeff would work out under the hoop for ten hours a day on weekends. During his high school days, there were only four days in four years when he didn't practice the game! Whenever practice started to get boring, Jeff would look for competition. If there weren't enough kids in the neighborhood for a tough game, he and his friends would cruise the streets in a car, looking for someone to play.

All that practice, plus the fact that he had grown to 6 feet, 11 inches, brought the college scouts pounding down Jeff's door. North Carolina's respected coach, Dean Smith, called Ruland the best big man to come out of high school since Bill Walton. Although he had his choice of more than 250 scholarship offers, Ruland selected little Iona College near New York City. Iona, with an enrollment of 5,500, had dreams of moving into the top ranks of college basketball, and their coach talked Jeff into joining the effort to make the Gaels a winning team.

Ruland kept his part of the bargain by leading the nation's freshmen in scoring (22.3) and rebounding (12.8). During his three-year stay at Iona, he led his team to such high points as a thrashing of powerful Kentucky and a 17-point victory over national champion Louisville.

But the national fame that Jeff had been promised at Iona didn't come about. The team never advanced far in the NCAA tournament and, with little coverage from the national press, Ruland never made first team All-American. Soured on the way things had turned out, Ruland signed with an agent after his junior year, which made him ineligible to play any more college ball. Jeff then put his name in the NBA draft, but his lack of recognition continued to haunt him. The man who was once compared to Bill Walton lasted until the second round, when he was claimed by Golden State. Even the Warriors

Jeff Ruland

weren't overly tickled to get Ruland and quickly traded him to Washington.

Insulted by the pros' lack of faith in him, Jeff turned his back on the NBA. Some thought he was ruining his future chances as a pro when he flew to Spain to play for a team in Barcelona. Although he led his team to the finals of the European Cup, it was a rough year for the American. Jealous teammates and rowdy fans took some of the fun out of playing. Ruland dreamed of coming back to the United States to prove how good he could be.

49

As it turned out, Jeff's year in Spain had been timed perfectly. While he was away, Washington's two most powerful players left the Bullets. Unseld retired and All-Star Elvin Hayes was traded to Houston, which left the team with a shortage of muscle. No one doubted that the 6-foot, 11-inch, 260-pound Ruland could ease the power shortage. But there were doubts that Jeff could overcome an unusual handicap: short arms. The big guy's arms were so stubby that he could reach no higher than some of the smaller forwards in the league.

Jeff showed, however, that he could use his huge body to keep longer-armed foes away from the ball. He also proved to be a splendid shooter who could move with surprising quickness. Most importantly, he was burning to prove that he could be a star.

At Washington, Ruland teamed with 6-foot, 9-inch, 240-pound Rick Mahorn in the Bullet front line. Opponents soon found that driving toward the basket against the Bullets was like trying to run into the middle of the Washington Redskins' defensive line. The two became known as the "Beef Brothers" as they fought for rebounds and set jarring picks for their teammates. Ruland was so difficult to get past that one player said he seemed to grow until he filled up the whole lane!

With his path barred by the massive Ruland, Cleveland's Larry Kenon decides this is a good time to pass off!

New York Knick forward Ernie Grunfeld will never agree that basketball is a non-contact sport! Here he becomes filler for a "Beef Brothers" sandwich, which jars the ball loose.

Another claimed it was lucky that Ruland had such tiny arms so that the rest of them at least had a chance to get a rebound.

On offense, Ruland would get his opponent off balance with his quick first step and then roar to the basket like a runaway boxcar. Bullying his way in for good shots, Jeff sank nearly 60 percent of them and scored 14.6 points as the Bullets' sixth man. His huge presence helped Washington overcome the loss of its former stars and made sure they were a respectable team.

In 1982-83, Ruland bloomed into a genuine star and finally got the recognition he had long been seeking. Firmly in place as the Bullets' starting center, he scored 19.4 points a game and finished eighth in rebounding with 11.0. By his third year in the league, he had become the best scorer/ rebounder since Moses Malone. Big Jeff ranked 3rd in the NBA in rebounding with a 12.3 average and 15th in scoring with 22.2 points per game. Opponents had discovered that when Jeff Ruland is playing, the basketball court suddenly seems very small.

Buck Williams, the most graceful of the strongmen in this book, picks off a layup attempt by Washington's John Lucas.

6
Buck
Williams

If you were to line up the New Jersey Nets to guess who was the team's most rugged rebounder, there's little doubt whom the choice would be. At 6 feet, 11 inches, and 260 well-muscled pounds, Darryl Dawkins may be the strongest and most famous bruiser in the game. But for all of his size, strength, and coordination, Dawkins doesn't come close to matching the rebounding efforts of Buck Williams. If Dawkins is like a sports car that turns heads with its flashes of brilliance, Williams is like the reliable family station wagon. Most of the time he does the job so well and so routinely that you don't even know he's there.

It has always been easy to overlook Charles Linwood Williams, who was born on March 8, 1960. The youngest of five children in his home in Rocky

Mount, North Carolina, he was often left to entertain himself and learned to make decisions for himself at an early age. That independence carried over into basketball. Halfway into his first high school basketball game, Buck had made up his mind about the style of game he would play. Others could dribble and shoot and pile up the points, but he was going after the rebounds.

Following in the footsteps of Rocky Mount native Phil Ford, a pro standout, Williams stubbornly stuck to his goal. Williams, whose boyhood nickname, "Hucklebuck," had been shortened to Buck, powered his team to the North Carolina State High School championship.

Living in the backyard of such basketball powerhouses as Duke and the University of North Carolina, Williams was expected to attend college in his home state. But Buck wasn't one to let others make decisions for him, and he shocked locals by going to North Carolina's arch-rival, the University of Maryland, instead. Not only did Buck move into enemy territory, he had also chosen a school that would give him no chance of being the star. That role would go to another Maryland recruit, Albert King, the most outstanding high school player in the country that year.

Charles "Buck" Williams

But as usual, Buck had everything planned out. It was just fine with him if King got all the attention; in fact, it was an advantage. While Albert had to worry about living up to his high school headlines, Buck was free to work on improving his game. He had studied the pros long enough to know that there was always a need for a good rebounder. If he could learn to control the backboards, the pros would find him, even if the fans didn't. Buck figured the pros would be on his doorstep, ready to sign him, by the end of his junior year.

At Maryland, the 6-foot, 8-inch, 215-pound Williams was asked to play the key position of center for a team that was expected to challenge for the national title. He never did score much, and every spring the Maryland Terrapins fizzled as a title contender. But beneath the disappointing scores, Williams was piling up some eye-popping statistics. Although three inches shorter than Duke's Mike Gminski and seven inches shorter than Virginia's Ralph Sampson, Buck outrebounded both future pros in conference play.

The pro draft following Buck's junior year proved Williams right. Pro teams were so desperate for a rebounding forward that the little-known Williams was the fifth man chosen in the 1981 draft. The New Jersey Nets selected Albert King in the draft as well as Williams, but this time it was Buck who had top billing. After receiving a few tips from master rebounder Maurice Lucas, who had played for the Nets the previous season, Williams was ready to take on the NBA giants.

The hard work and lessons of many years of battling larger centers paid off at once. Now at his natural position of power forward, Buck was able to flex his muscles. With his many head fakes, his great leaping ability, and his strength, Buck kept

In a vivid demonstration of why it takes more than height and leaping ability to grab rebounds, Williams uses every muscle to keep Milwaukee's tall Harvey Catchings away from the ball.

edging out his more experienced opponents in the rebounding department. At the end of the year, Buck ranked third in the NBA in rebounding with a 12.3 average.

Williams taps in a shot against Jack Sikma. It was Buck's tough inside play that helped to make the New Jersey Nets a contender.

Williams also threw in a surprise for his coaches by scoring more than 15 points per game. Although rookies such as Isiah Thomas and Mark Aguirre won far more fans, it was Williams who was named an NBA All-Star and the league's Rookie of the Year.

In 1982-83, Williams shifted his goals toward something other than rebounding and worked at driving more to the basket and sharpening his shooting skills. The effort paid off as Williams tied Albert King as the Nets' leading scorer, averaging 17 points per game.

But still, whenever anyone thought of Buck Williams, they thought of rebounding. That season, he finished second in the NBA in that department and was the only player besides Moses Malone to grab more than 1,000 rebounds. The next season, Buck again came in number two to Moses in rebounding average. With Malone's total playing time limited by injuries, however, jumping-jack Williams finished the season as the NBA's only 1,000-plus rebound man. Although he had become one of the Nets' top scoring threats, for Buck the name of the game was still, "follow the bouncing ball!"

Although often outnumbered and overmatched against larger foes,
Dan Roundfield never backs away.

7
Dan Roundfield

While Buck Williams became a rebounder by choice, Dan Roundfield rebounded out of sheer frustration. Born in Detroit, Michigan, in 1953, Roundfield at first put all his energy into baseball. It wasn't until the 11th grade when he sprouted to 6 feet, 3 inches that he thought of trying basketball.

Detroit's Chadsey High School was no place for a beginner. The high school system that had sent George Gervin on his way to stardom was full of talented players. To make matters worse, the inexperienced Roundfield was put at center, where he had to battle players taller than himself in every game. Poor Dan was nearly trampled into the court during his first year. He could not look to his teammates for help, either. Dan struggled to get position against larger, more skilled centers, but he could just as well have saved his strength as his teammates weren't about to pass the ball to this overmatched newcomer. Dan decided that if he wanted to touch the basketball, he would have to grab some rebounds.

That first year was a painful learning process, and Roundfield's team went through an entire season without winning a game. Although Dan improved during his final year of high school, he didn't know if he should try to keep playing or not. Even his coach advised him to give up the game because he thought Dan wasn't likely to amount to anything.

Dan finally decided that he could at least try to continue at a small school, so he enrolled at Central Michigan University. The thin, 6-foot, 8-inch forward began to put on some muscle, which helped him to hold his ground near the basket. By 1975, he had made such progress that he led his team to the conference championship. Then in the Mideast Regional of the NCAA Tournament, he showed he could play against the larger schools. In one game against highly rated Kentucky, he blocked eight shots. Officials were so impressed that they named him co-winner of the region's Most

Valuable Player Award (with Indiana's Kent Benson).

The honor got the Indiana Pacers excited enough to draft Roundfield in the first round in 1975. By the end of training camp, however, they weren't as thrilled with their selection, and their unimpressive rookie spent most of his first year warming the bench.

Roundfield saw much more action during his second year with the Pacers, but he wasn't sure that was a. blessing, either. With regular center Len Elmore hurt, Dan was put in at center instead of his natural forward spot. The 6-foot, 8-inch, 205-pounder had no business taking on such giants as Artis Gilmore and Kareem Abdul-Jabbar. But that situation was no different than what Dan had gone through in high school. He simply buckled down, played as hard as he could, and somehow averaged 13.9 points and more than eight rebounds per game.

For Dan it must have felt like being let out of prison when he was put back at power forward in 1977-78. There he used his long arms, leaping skill, and upper body strength to grab over 10 rebounds per game. Then after playing out his contract with Indiana that year, he found the Atlanta Hawks eager to sign him.

Roundfield reminds Philadelphia's Bobby Jones that the Hawks' top rebounder also knows how to shoot.

During his first year in Atlanta, Dan gave the Hawks more than their money's worth. He scored 15.3 points per game and took 10.8 rebounds per contest to earn the team's Most Valuable Player Award. Although not blessed with the massive shoulders of many rebounders, Dan was stronger than he looked, and he used every ounce of strength that he had. Crashing elbow to elbow with the bruisers, Roundfield's body lost many battles. His front teeth were knocked out in a college game, and he wore plenty of tape on the wrists that had been broken four times. Dan's back sometimes bothered him so much that he couldn't bend at the free throw line, and he had to wear a mask to protect an injury to his face in 1983-84.

Through it all, however, Roundfield continued to win the battle of the statistics. In 1979-80, he kept his average at over 10 rebounds per game while boosting his scoring to 16.5 points. During the All-Star game that season, he came away grinning from his matches with the NBA's best big men. Playing in just over half the game, Roundfield outrebounded everyone, pulling in 13 and adding 18 points. In 1981-82, he enjoyed his finest season yet, with an 18.6 scoring average and 11.7 rebounds per game.

Dan Roundfield

The Hawks' ace was even more valuable than the statistics showed. In fact, the best part of his game didn't even show up in the box score. With his long arms and leaping skill always putting him near the leaders in blocked shots, many coaches argue that Dan is the best defensive forward in the pros. He was such a hard worker that opponents got worn out trying to work around him for a shot.

With Roundfield barring the way, Washington's Tom McMillen finds there is no easy path to the basket.

Unfortunately for Dan, it takes more than tireless effort to win championships. It also takes teammates. Faced with the burden of playing for very average Atlanta teams, Dan wound up with few wins for his trouble. Then, following another dreary Atlanta season in 1983-84, Roundfield was traded to the Detroit Pistons for Antoine Carr, a young power forward. With a chance to blend his talents with those of All-Pros such as Isiah Thomas and Kelly Tripuka, Dan finally hoped to get a chance to battle for an NBA championship. At the very least, he would get to demonstrate to his hometown Detroit fans that the hopeless high school center had really amounted to something.

8
Terry Cummings

No one can accuse Terry Cummings of living a dull life. An ex-ghetto hood who became an ordained minister, Cummings is one of the hardest-working, most courageous men in sports. Yet he may not have the heart to play pro basketball. In an age where drugs have ruined many athletes' lives, Cummings owes his career and probably his life to drugs. Most incredible of all, it took him five years to move from a beginning basketball player to being the best *rookie* the NBA had seen in nearly 15 years.

It all started back in Hammond, Indiana, in 1961 where Terry was the fifth of 13 children born to John and Verda Cummings. The family moved to Chicago while Terry was young. There he and his brothers followed every move of their hero,

Terry Cummings is too quick for some players (as he proves here to Houston's Caldwell Jones), too strong for others, and too talented for anyone to stop.

Stan Mikita, and the rest of the Chicago Black Hawks hockey club. Their goal was to become the world's first black hockey team.

One brother, however, shifted his sights to basketball. He would wake up early and trudge over to the park at 6:00 A.M. to practice. Sometimes younger brother Terry would tag along, but the little guy never had a chance because his brother outplayed him badly every time. Terry then drifted away from sports into some bad company, which was easy to do in a neighborhood so rough that Cummings carried a gun as early as the seventh grade. It seemed that if there were a way to get into trouble, Terry could find it. He argued with his dad, broke into cars and safes, joined gang fights, and cut or flunked classes.

Then, overnight, the troublesome boy changed into a dedicated, law-abiding student. At the age of 16, Terry had a dream that frightened him into changing his ways. Now deeply religious, he was so confident his life had changed for the better that he carried his Bible through the toughest neighborhoods.

Looking for good ways to spend his energy, Cummings tried out for his high school basketball team for a second time. As a freshman, he had made a half-hearted effort to make the team but had been cut from the squad. This time the "new" Terry Cummings took to the game as if *he* were the veteran and everyone else was new at it. Within two years, nearly every college in the United States with a gymnasium offered him a basketball scholarship. Terry decided to stay in Chicago and play for DePaul University. Determined to make a success of himself, he cleaned streets and drove a truck to earn money, he got married, and he became an ordained minister. In his "spare time," Cummings scored 14.2 points and averaged 9.4 rebounds for a highly-rated DePaul team.

During his sophomore year, Terry ran into a team situation so bad that even his cheerful, energetic nature couldn't handle it. DePaul was led by the tremendously talented Mark Aguirre, who totally dominated the Blue Demon offense. DePaul stopped playing as a team, and Terry could not figure out what his role should be. His play suffered, and he became so discouraged that he nearly quit to become a full-time minister.

When Aguirre left after that season to join the pros, Terry was called on to be the leader. It was a role he enjoyed. He always had time for people, and he worked to fit his talents to those of the

Terry Cummings

team. Yet when DePaul fell behind near the end of a game, it was the 6-foot, 9-inch, 220-pound forward who would suddenly take over and pour in enough points to get the victory. With Terry leading the way, DePaul's Blue Demons posted a surprising 27-2 record.

As with several others in this book, Cummings went on to the pros before his senior year. Although many pro fans had heard little about him, he was the second man chosen in the draft, right after North Carolina's James Worthy. Cummings' new team, the San Diego (now Los Angeles) Clippers, thought it might take some time before their inexperienced rookie could adjust to the rougher pro game. But they should have suspected that Terry was anything but ordinary. After missing all of training camp and the first four games of the season in a contract struggle, Terry came back to score 19 points in his first game. When he scored 32 and grabbed 24 rebounds in his third game, the Clippers realized they had a better player than they had ever dreamed.

San Diego floundered in their usual spot near the bottom of the standings that year, but Cummings had rival coaches shaking their heads in awe. As in college, Cummings simply took over in the final minutes of a close game. Had the Clippers stayed close to their opponents more often, Cummings might have bettered their 25-57 mark.

Terry gave his team nearly as many scares, as thrills, however. In a December 15 game, he collapsed on the court without any warning. Doctors suspected he was suffering from a shortage of iron in his diet, and they let him work himself back into the lineup. Then in March, the Clipper star began to have trouble catching his breath. Concerned team doctors outfitted him with a device that would monitor his heart while he was playing.

Realizing this November 6, 1982, game is Cumming's first start as a pro, Mark Olberding and his Chicago teammates wonder how good Terry will be once he gains some experience.

When two powerful rivals such as Cummings and Buck Williams lock on to the ball at the same time, everyone else, including New Jersey's Albert King, had better back off!

What they discovered in an April 5 game was like something out of a science fiction story: During play, Cummings' heart rate skyrocketed to a deadly 300 beats per minute! San Diego immediately pulled him from the lineup and tried to find the problem. It turned out that Terry had a serious heart condition. The promising career of the NBA's first rookie since 1969 to rank in the top ten in both scoring and rebounding seemed over. But careful treatment with drugs settled Terry's heart, and he decided to continue in pro ball.

Despite all he had been through, Cummings' life was unchanged in 1983-84. He still forced his way to the hoop to score over 20 points per game and to grab crucial rebounds. His efforts, however, did nothing to shake San Diego out of its last-place rut. When the Clippers decided to make drastic moves after the season, they discovered that Terry Cummings was worth a fortune. The Milwaukee Bucks outbid a host of trading rivals, offering star forward Marques Johnson and proven veterans Junior Bridgeman and Harvey Catchings for Cummings and two reserves.

Terry was delighted to return to Milwaukee, so near to the place where that competitive fire had been lit in him at the age of 16. He was eager to prove to the Bucks that the fire was still burning strong.

ACKNOWLEDGMENTS: The photographs are reproduced through the courtesy of: pp. 4, 7, 13, 18, 25, 28, 33, 34, 46, 51, 52, 54, 60, 69, 72, 78, AP/Wide World Photos; pp. 8, 41, 77, UP/Bettmann Archive; pp. 15, 16, Philadelphia 76ers; p. 22, Portland Trailblazers; p. 24, Phoenix Suns; p. 31, Seattle Supersonics; pp. 36, 39, 43, Utah Jazz; p. 49, Washington Bullets; pp. 57, 59 (Al Kooistra), New Jersey Nets; p. 62, Indiana Pacers; pp. 66, 68, Atlanta Hawks; p. 75, Los Angeles Clippers. Cover photograph courtesy of the Utah Jazz.

80